GREAT PLANET EARTH SEARCH

Emma Helbrough

Illustrated by Ian Jackson

Designed by Stephen Wright

Edited by Anna Milbourne
Geography consultant: Dr. Roger Trend
Wildlife consultants: Dr. Margaret Rostron
and Dr. John Rostron

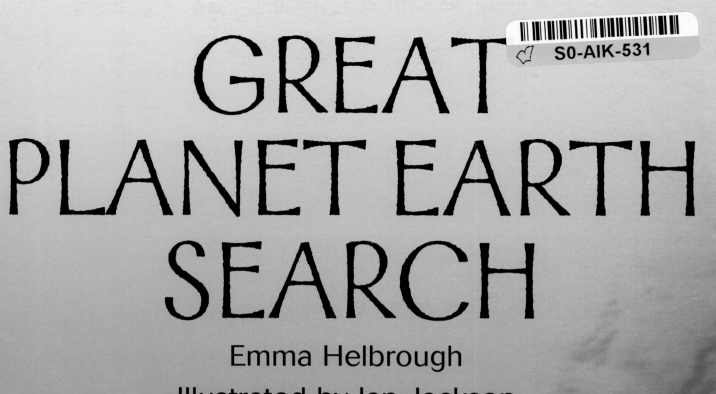

Contents

About this book

This puzzle book is filled with pictures of all kinds of places around the world, from deserts to rainforests. There are lots of things for you to spot in each picture. Can you find them all? If you get stuck, the answers are on pages 28–31. The example pages below show you how each puzzle works.

A red square on the globe in the corner of the page shows you where in the world the scene is set.

Each little picture shows you what to look for in the big picture.

The writing next to each little picture tells you how many of that thing you need to find.

You will have to look hard to spot these iris flowers in the distance.

This salamander is partly hidden, but don't miss it out.

Winding river

High up in the mountains, rain and melted snow make streams, which join together to make rivers. Rivers flow downhill, winding across the land until they flow into a lake or reach the sea.

Rivers like this flow into the Great Lakes in Canada.

Spot 5 green darner dragonflies.

An oxbow lake forms when a bend in a river becomes cut off from the river. Find 1.

Wood ducks tip upside down in the water to feed on water plants. Spot 7

Painted turtles often sunbathe on logs or rocks. Can you find 6 more?

Spot 2 bridges.

River otters have sleek, waterproof fur and short, powerful legs to help them swim. Find 10.

At a water mill, the river turns a wheel, which powers a machine that grinds grain into flour. Find 1 water mill.

Yellow-spotted salamanders visit rivers to lay their eggs. Can you find 3 salamanders?

Spot 2 canoes.

Water lilies have big leaves that float on the water's surface. Find 15 water lily leaves.

Spot 5 brook silverside fish leaping out of the water.

Great blue herons wade in rivers, catching fish, frogs and insects to eat. Spot 5.

Blue flag irises grow along riverbanks. Can you find 21 more iris flowers.

24

25

To make the puzzles more fun, each big picture shows lots of things to spot very close together. In real life, these places are much less crowded.

Planet Earth

Earth is one of nine planets that travel around, or orbit, the Sun. It has many amazing features, from snow-capped mountains to dark, underground caves. It is the only planet where we know that plants and animals live.

World climates

Earth is a place of extremes. It can be freezing cold in the Arctic and extremely hot at the Equator. Which kinds of plants and animals live in an area depends on the weather the area usually has, known as its climate. In this book, you can explore places with many different climates. If you look back at this map, you can find out where else in the world has a similar climate.

pages 12–13

NORTH AMERICA

pages 16–17

pages 24–25

pages 14–15

Atlan Ocea

pages 18–19

SOUTH AMERICA

Climate key

This shows which different climates the shading on the map represents:

Mountains – cold for much of the year

Polar climate – very cold all year

Temperate climate – some rain in all seasons

Warm climate – summers are hot and dry, winters are mild and wet

Desert climate – hot and very dry all year

Tropical climate – hot all year, with heavy rain in the wet season

Equatorial climate – hot and wet, with heavy rain

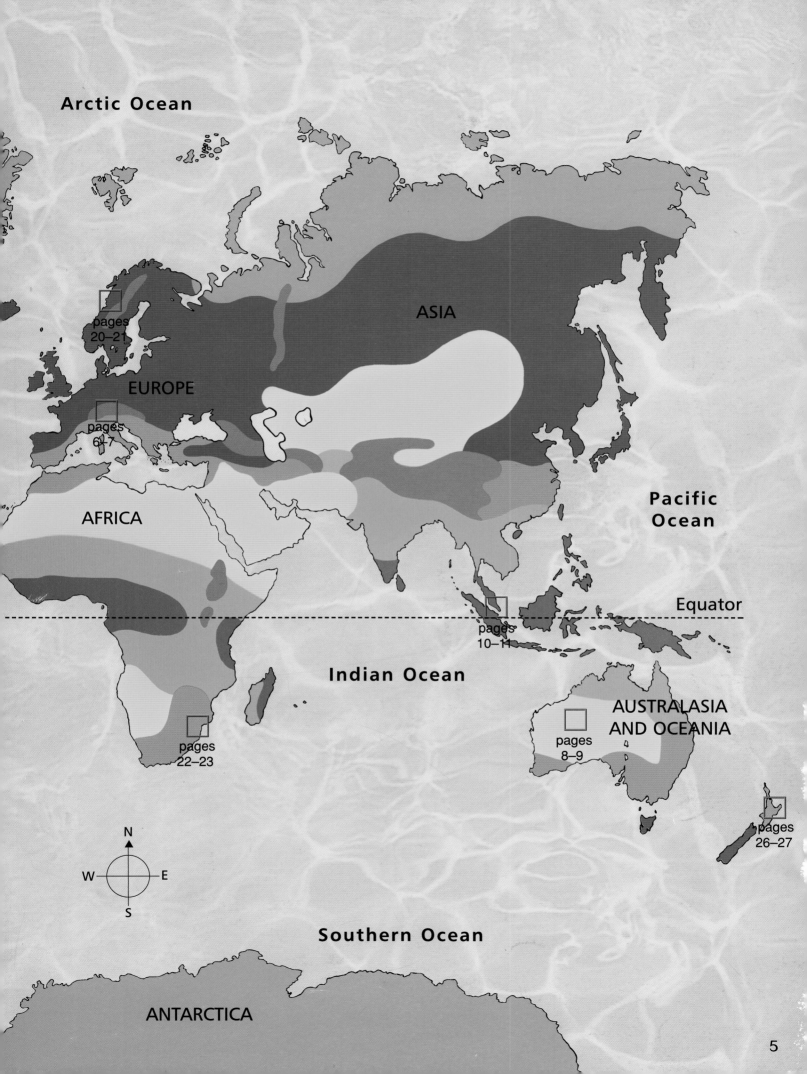

Arctic Ocean

ASIA

EUROPE

pages
20–21

pages
6–7

AFRICA

Pacific
Ocean

Equator

pages
10–11

Indian Ocean

AUSTRALASIA
AND OCEANIA

pages
8–9

pages
22–23

N

W   E

S

pages
26–27

Southern Ocean

ANTARCTICA

5

Alpine slopes

It's much colder and windier on the higher Alpine slopes than in the valleys below. Many mountain animals have thick fur to keep them warm. Even plants have adapted to living in cold surroundings.

The Alps are the highest mountains in Europe.

Many mountain peaks are covered in snow all year round. Find 6 snowy peaks.

Wallcreepers search for small insects to eat. Spot 3 wallcreepers.

Edelweiss plants have furry leaves to protect them from the cold. Find 10 edelweiss flowers.

Alpine hares have brown fur in summer and white fur in winter. This makes them hard for predators to spot all year round. Spot 12 more Alpine hares.

A glacier is a river of ice that slides slowly downhill. Can you find 2 glaciers?

Mountain houses, or chalets, have steep roofs and overhanging eaves. Spot 16 chalets.

Spot 8 purple-shot copper butterflies.

Cable cars carry people up and down the slopes. Find 5.

Golden eagles circle in the air, looking for hares to eat. Spot 3 golden eagles.

Can you see 6 hot-air balloons?

Cumulus clouds have flat bottoms and puffy tops. Find 9.

Alpine ibexes climb about on rocky mountain slopes to graze. Spot 18.

Gliders don't have engines. They use the wind to help them fly. Find 2.

Spruce trees grow low down on the slopes. Higher up, it is too cold and windy for them. Spot 15.

Australian desert

Deserts are the driest places on Earth. Most are baking hot during the day and freezing cold at night.

Few animals and plants live in deserts because there is little water or shelter for them.

Deserts cover most of central Australia.

Tumbleweed plants scatter seeds as they are blown along by the wind. Spot 9.

Baobab trees store water in their swollen, barrel-like trunks. Can you find 5 more?

A dust devil is a moving spiral of air and dust. Spot 1.

Kangaroos can't walk. They hop everywhere, using their tails to balance. Find 6.

A mesa is an isolated hill with steep sides and a flat top. Spot 4 mesas.

Bushfires often start when lightning strikes plants or trees. Find 1 bushfire.

An oasis is a fertile area of a desert, where water is found. Spot 2 oases.

Emus are flightless birds. Find 5.

Woma pythons hunt for lizards, birds and small animals to eat. Spot 4.

Spot 5 tents.

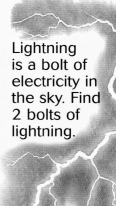

Lightning is a bolt of electricity in the sky. Find 2 bolts of lightning.

Thorny devils look fierce, but really they're harmless. Their spikes protect them from attackers. Spot 3 more thorny devils.

The Aboriginal people of Australia make hand prints on rocks that are sacred to them. Spot 5 more hand prints.

Mangrove swamp

Mangroves are trees that grow along tropical shores where rivers meet the sea. The water is a mix of fresh water from the river and salt water from the sea. Mangroves have adapted to grow in salty wat...

Mangrove swamps are found along the coasts of southeast Asia.

Mangrove seedlings drop into the water and float until they reach mud banks, where they take root. Find 29.

Male fiddler crabs have one claw bigger than the other. They use their big claws to fight over females. Spot 6 males.

Hawksbill turtles use their sharp, beaky mouths to break open shellfish. Spot 2 more.

Mudskippers are fish that can breathe both in and out of water. They use their fins to climb onto mangrove roots. Find 9.

Spot 7 oysters.

Saltwater crocodiles sometimes leap out of the water to catch birds. Spot 2 crocodile...

10

Mangrove trees have unusual, stilt-like roots, which stop their trunks from toppling over in the mud. Find 5 more mangrove trees.

Little egrets roost in mangroves. When the tide is out, they wade in the shallow water and catch fish. Spot 3 little egrets.

Cownose rays usually swim near the surface, but sink to the bottom to hunt for clams. Can you spot 10?

Fishermen build huts on stilts in the sea. They tie their fishing nets to the stilts. Can you find 1 hut?

People use kayaks to explore the mangroves without disturbing the wildlife. Find 3 kayaks.

Silver moony fish hide from danger among the mangrove roots. Spot 15 more.

Banded sea kraits swim underwater, but come to the surface to breathe. Spot 6.

Icy Arctic

The temperature in Greenland is usually well below freezing, and in winter the surface of the sea freezes over, forming a layer of sea ice. In this picture, it is spring and most of the sea ice has melted.

Greenland is a large island in the Arctic Ocean.

People use snowmobiles to explore the icy landscape. Spot 2 snowmobiles.

Lemmings use their claws like shovels to burrow into the snow. Spot 3 lemmings.

Some people travel around on sleds pulled by husky dogs. Find 1 sled pulled by dogs.

Spot 12 walruses.

Most goods are flown into villages, because Greenland doesn't have many roads. Spot 1 cargo plane.

Polar bears have very thick fur to keep them warm. Can you see 2 more adults and 2 cubs?

Unlike other owls, snowy owls hunt during the day. They catch small birds and lemmings. Find 3 more snowy owls.

Male narwhals have a long, pointed tusk. Spot 2 narwhals.

Arctic foxes hunt lemmings. They pound the snow with their paws to break into their burrows. Find 3 Arctic foxes.

Musk oxen have long, woolly fur that hangs almost to their feet. Spot 6.

An iceberg is a chunk of ice floating in the sea. You can only see one seventh of an iceberg above water. Spot 7 icebergs.

Most Greenlanders live along the coast, in small villages of brightly painted wooden houses. Spot 11 wooden houses.

Caribou eat plants called lichens in winter. They sniff them out under the snow. Can you find 12 more caribou?

Limestone cave

Limestone is a type of rock that wears away easily. When rain seeps into cracks in limestone, the cracks slowly widen. Over thousands of years, large underground caves can develop.

Limestone caves like this are found in Missouri, USA.

Ferns need sunlight to make their food, so they only grow where light shines. Find 5.

A sink-hole is a hole in the roof of a cave, which lets sunlight in. Spot 3 sink-holes.

Snakes sometimes fall through sink-holes into caves. Spot 4 rat snakes.

Find 10 cave crickets.

As water splashes onto the cave floor, it deposits minerals, which slowly build up into cone shapes called stalagmites. Spot 32 more stalagmites.

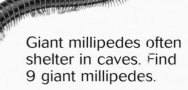

Giant millipedes often shelter in caves. Find 9 giant millipedes.

As water drips through the cave roof, it leaves behind minerals. Over time, the minerals build up into icicle shapes called stalactites. Spot 29 stalactites.

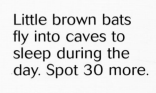

Little brown bats fly into caves to sleep during the day. Spot 30 more.

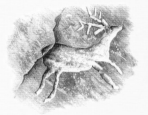

Early humans carved pictures of the animals they hunted in rock. Can you see 8 deer pictures?

When a stalactite meets a stalagmite, they join to form a column. Find 4 columns.

Fossils are the remains of dead animals and plants that have slowly turned to rock. Spot 5 crinoid fossils.

Black bear cubs are born in caves. They stay inside until they are a few months old. Find 3 bear cubs.

Cave salamanders make their homes in damp, dark caves. Can you see 8?

15

Wheat fields

Wheat is a type of grass that is farmed in many parts of the world. It is a very useful plant. The grain is ground into flour and the dry stalks, called straw, are used as cattle bedding.

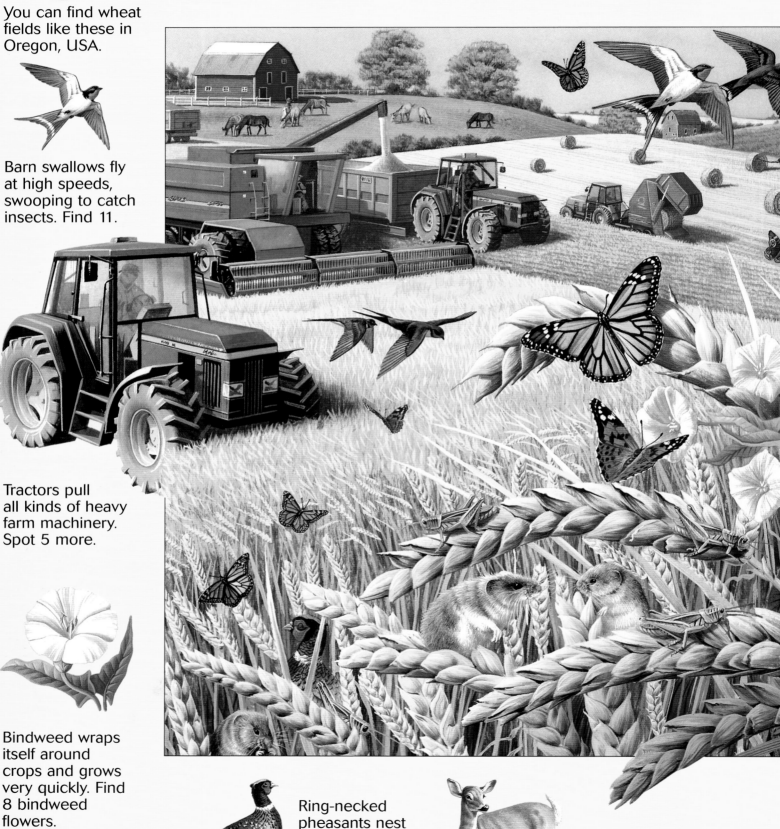

USA

You can find wheat fields like these in Oregon, USA.

Barn swallows fly at high speeds, swooping to catch insects. Find 11.

Tractors pull all kinds of heavy farm machinery. Spot 5 more.

Bindweed wraps itself around crops and grows very quickly. Find 8 bindweed flowers.

Ring-necked pheasants nest on the ground in wheat fields. Spot 3.

Hungry white-tailed deer sometimes wander into fields to nibble the wheat. Can you find 1?

Can you see 9 monarch butterflies?

Combine harvesters cut down wheat and separate the grain from the straw. Spot 2.

Grain is dropped from a combine harvester into a grain trailer. Spot 3 grain trailers.

Baling machines gather up straw and roll it into bales. Spot 2 bailing machines.

Grasshoppers eat all kinds of plants, including wheat. Find 7.

Spot 12 straw bales.

Farmers use barns to keep cattle in or to store grain or farm machinery. Spot 3 barns.

Young fieldmice climb wheat stalks to collect grain to eat. Can you see 6 more fieldmice?

Tropical rainforest

In hot, steamy rainforests, some trees grow very tall. Many animals, and even some plants, live high up in the trees because there is more light there than on the ground. This area is called the canopy.

Tamanduas spend most of their time in trees, searching for ants to eat. Spot 4.

Golden eyelash vipers slither along branches in the canopy. Find 3.

Spot 7 more blue morpho butterflies.

Can you find 6 red-eyed

Central America

Tropical rainforests cover many parts of Central America.

Some orchids grow on trees. Their roots soak up moisture from the air. Find 20 orchid flowers.

Capuchin monkeys use their tails to grab branches as they swing from tree

Toucans aren't very good at flying. They hop from tree to tree, looking for fruit. Spot 5.

Scientists hide in tree houses to study rainforest plants and animals. Can you find 2 tree houses?

Monkey-ladder vines have thick stems and hang from branches high in the canopy. Spot 5.

People explore the canopy using treetop walkways. Find 3 walkways.

Strawberry poison-dart frogs have red and blue skin. This warns attackers that they are poisonous. Find 7 more.

A waterfall is a sudden, vertical drop in a river as it plunges over a steep hillside. Spot 1.

Tank plants grow in cracks on trees. They trap the water they need inside their tightly packed leaves. Spot 4 more.

Craggy coast

Coastlines are constantly changing shape. Powerful waves gradually wear away some parts of the cliffs, while in other places, pieces of worn-away rock are washed ashore, forming beaches.

Northern Europe is known for its rugged coastlines.

Wind turbines turn wind energy into electricity. Find 8.

Can you spot 18 herring gulls?

Lighthouses flash to warn ships about dangerous coastlines. Spot 1 lighthouse.

Atlantic puffins spend most of the year far out at sea. They only come ashore to nest. Find 8 more.

A trawler is powered by a motor. This turns a propeller, which pushes the boat forward. Spot 4 trawlers.

Killer whales hunt for fish, squid, sea birds and sharks. Can you spot 6?

Spot 2 hang-gliders soaring on the wind.

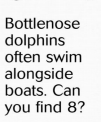

Bottlenose dolphins often swim alongside boats. Can you find 8?

Mooring buoys are anchored to the sea bed. People tie their boats to them. Find 5 mooring buoys.

Seals have a layer of fat under their skin which keeps them warm in icy water. Spot 5.

Yachts are pushed through the water by the wind blowing against their sails. Spot 10.

As waves crash against the cliffs, they carve arches out of the rock. Can you see 2 arches?

A stack is a pillar of rock in the sea. A stack is formed when the middle of an arch collapses. Find 5 stacks.

African grasslands

Grasslands are open areas of land covered in many different types of grasses. Because of the abundance of grasses, they attract plant-eating animals, which in turn attract meat-eaters.

Grasslands like this are found in southern Africa.

Spot 12 African elephants.

Insects called termites live in mounds, which they build out of mud and saliva. Can you spot 8 termite mounds?

Springboks spring into the air when they are afraid, which is how they got their name. Find 24.

A giraffe's long neck helps it to reach the leaves of acacia trees. Spot 10 more giraffes.

Vultures fly over grasslands, searching for dead animals to eat. Spot 4 vultures.

Raised rocky areas called koppies make good resting spots for lions. Find two lions on a koppie.

People watch animals from safari trucks. Spot 3 trucks.

Masked weaverbirds build onion-shaped nests out of blades of grass. Find 4 weaverbird nests.

Acacia trees provide food and shelter for zebras, birds and many other animals. Spot 8 more acacia trees.

Zebras live in groups, so that some can watch out for predators while others eat, drink or rest. Can you spot 12 zebras?

Animals gather at water holes to drink. Find 3 water holes.

Warthogs keep cool by wallowing in water holes. Spot 7 warthogs.

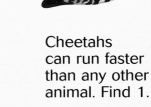

Cheetahs can run faster than any other animal. Find 1.

23

Winding river

High up in the mountains, rain and melted snow make streams, which join together to make rivers. Rivers flow downhill, winding across the land until they flow into a lake or reach the sea.

Canada

Rivers like this flow into the Great Lakes in Canada.

Spot 5 green darner dragonflies.

An oxbow lake forms when a bend in a river becomes cut off from the river. Find 1.

Wood ducks tip upside down in the water to feed on water plants. Spot 7.

Painted turtles often sunbathe on logs or rocks. Can you find 6 more?

Spot 2 bridges.

Yellow-spotted salamanders visit rivers to lay their eggs. Can you find 3 salamanders?

Spot 2 canoes.

Water lilies have big leaves that float on the water's surface. Find 15 water lily leaves.

Spot 5 brook silverside fish leaping out of the water.

Great blue herons wade in rivers, catching fish, frogs and insects to eat. Spot 5.

Blue flag irises grow along riverbanks. Can you find 21 more iris flowers?

River otters have sleek, waterproof fur and short, powerful legs to help them swim. Find 10.

At a water mill, the river turns a wheel, which powers a machine that grinds grain into flour. Find 1 water mill.

25

Hot spots

Beneath the surface of the Earth, there is a mass of hot, liquid rock. In volcanic areas, this can seep up through the ground, causing volcanoes and other dramatic natural features.

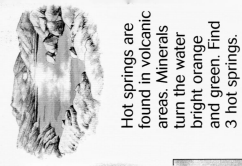

New Zealand is well-known for its volcanic areas.

Hot springs are found in volcanic areas. Minerals turn the water bright orange and green. Find 3 hot springs.

New Zealand falcons live in pine forests near the hot springs. Spot 2.

Mud pots are bubbling pools of runny mud. The bubbles are volcanic gases escaping from underground.

Mud volcanoes are small, cone-shaped mounds that ooze mud, clay and volcanic gases. Find 3.

Can you find 5 New Zealand

Sometimes, when the sun shines through steam spurting from a geyser, a rainbow forms. Spot 1 rainbow.

Find 5 tourists taking photographs.

A geyser is a jet of hot water and steam that shoots into the air from a hole in the ground. Spot 1 more geyser.

You can see a dramatic view of the volcanic landscape from a helicopter. Spot 2 helicopters.

Volcanic gases from deep under the ground escape through vents called fumaroles. Spot 12 fumaroles.

New Zealand's rugged terrain is ideal for mountain biking. Spot 4 cyclists.

Answers

The keys on the next few pages show you exactly where to find all the animals, plants and other things to spot in the big scenes. You can use these keys to check your answers, or to help you if you have a problem finding anything.

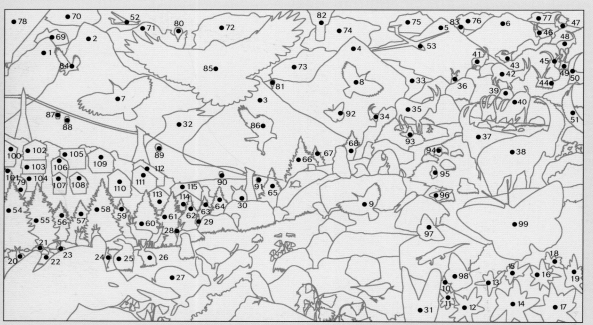

Alpine slopes 6–7

Snowy peaks, 1, 2, 3, 4, 5, 6
Wallcreepers, 7, 8, 9
Edelweiss flowers, 10, 11, 12, 13, 14, 15, 16, 17, 18, 19
Alpine hares, 20, 21, 22, 23, 24, 25, 26, 27, 28, 29, 30, 31
Glaciers, 32, 33
Alpine ibexes, 34, 35, 36, 37, 38, 39, 40, 41, 42, 43, 44, 45, 46, 47, 48, 49, 50, 51
Gliders, 52, 53
Spruce trees, 54, 55, 56, 57, 58, 59, 60, 61, 62, 63, 64, 65, 66, 67, 68
Cumulus clouds, 69, 70, 71, 72, 73, 74, 75, 76, 77
Hot-air balloons, 78, 79, 80, 81, 82, 83
Golden eagles, 84, 85, 86
Cable cars, 87, 88, 89, 90, 91
Purple-shot copper butterflies, 92, 93, 94, 95, 96, 97, 98, 99
Chalets, 100, 101, 102, 103, 104, 105, 106, 107, 108, 109, 110, 111, 112, 113, 114, 115

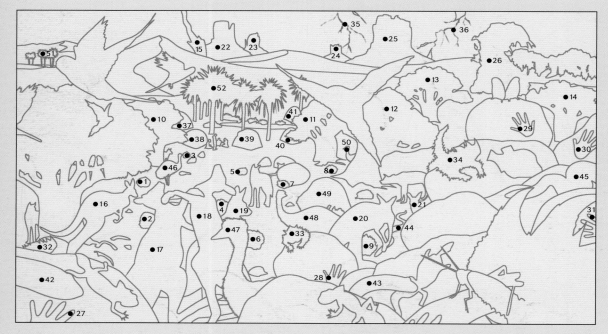

Australian desert 8–9

Tumbleweed plants, 1, 2, 3, 4, 5, 6, 7, 8, 9
Baobab trees, 10, 11, 12, 13, 14
Dust devil, 15
Kangaroos, 16, 17, 18, 19, 20, 21
Mesas, 22, 23, 24, 25
Bushfire, 26
Hand prints, 27, 28, 29, 30, 31
Thorny devils, 32, 33, 34
Bolts of lightning, 35, 36
Tents, 37, 38, 39, 40, 41
Woma pythons, 42, 43, 44, 45
Emus, 46, 47, 48, 49, 50
Oases, 51, 52

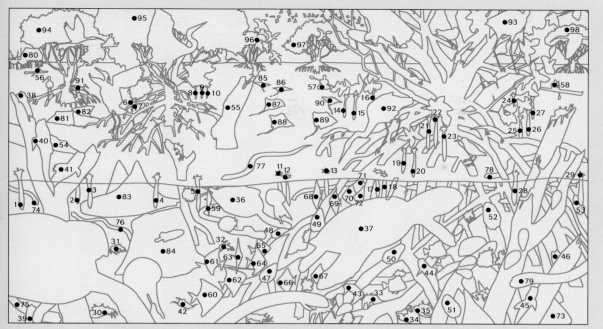

Mangrove swamp 10–11

Mangrove seedlings, 1, 2, 3, 4, 5, 6, 7, 8, 9, 10, 11, 12, 13, 14, 15, 16, 17, 18, 19, 20, 21, 22, 23, 24, 25, 26, 27, 28, 29
Male fiddler crabs, 30, 31, 32, 33, 34, 35
Hawksbill turtles, 36, 37
Mudskippers, 38, 39, 40, 41, 42, 43, 44, 45, 46
Oysters, 47, 48, 49, 50, 51, 52, 53
Saltwater crocodiles, 54, 55
Kayaks, 56, 57, 58
Silver moony fish, 59, 60, 61, 62, 63, 64, 65, 66, 67, 68, 69, 70, 71, 72, 73
Banded sea kraits, 74, 75, 76, 77, 78, 79
Hut on stilts, 80
Cownose rays, 81, 82, 83, 84, 85, 86, 87, 88, 89, 90
Little egrets, 91, 92, 93
Mangrove trees, 94, 95, 96, 97, 98

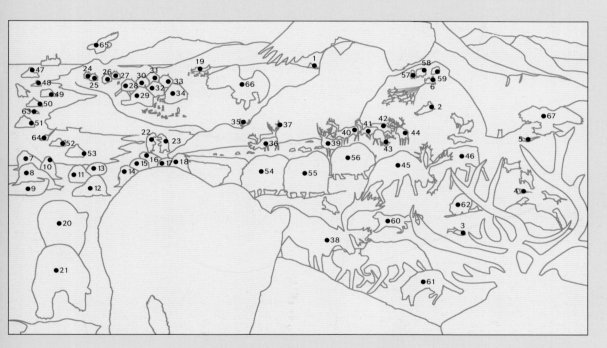

Icy Arctic 12–13

Snowmobiles, 1, 2
Lemmings, 3, 4, 5
Sled pulled by husky dogs, 6
Walruses, 7, 8, 9, 10, 11, 12, 13, 14, 15, 16, 17, 18
Cargo plane, 19
Polar bears, 20, 21, 22, 23
Houses, 24, 25, 26, 27, 28, 29, 30, 31, 32, 33, 34
Caribou, 35, 36, 37, 38, 39, 40, 41, 42, 43, 44, 45, 46
Icebergs, 47, 48, 49, 50, 51, 52, 53
Musk oxen, 54, 55, 56, 57, 58, 59
Arctic foxes, 60, 61, 62
Narwhals, 63, 64
Snowy owls, 65, 66, 67

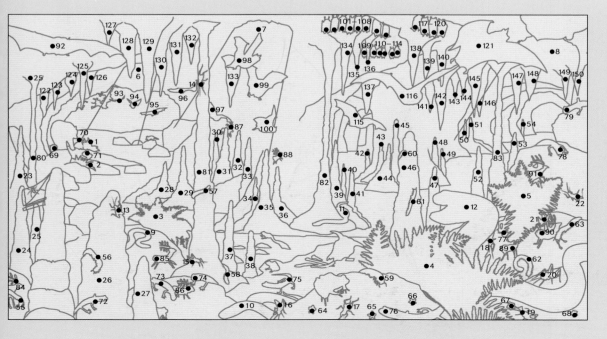

Limestone cave 14–15

Ferns, 1, 2, 3, 4, 5
Sink-holes, 6, 7, 8
Rat snakes, 9, 10, 11, 12
Cave crickets, 13, 14, 15, 16, 17, 18, 19, 20, 21, 22
Stalagmites, 23, 24, 25, 26, 27, 28, 29, 30, 31, 32, 33, 34, 35, 36, 37, 38, 39, 40, 41, 42, 43, 44, 45, 46, 47, 48, 49, 50, 51, 52, 53, 54
Giant millipedes, 55, 56, 57, 58, 59, 60, 61, 62, 63
Fossils, 64, 65, 66, 67, 68
Black bear cubs, 69, 70, 71
Cave salamanders, 72, 73, 74, 75, 76, 77, 78, 79
Columns, 80, 81, 82, 83
Deer pictures, 84, 85, 86, 87, 88, 89, 90, 91
Little brown bats, 92, 93, 94, 95, 96, 97, 98, 99, 100, 101, 102, 103, 104, 105, 106, 107, 108, 109, 110, 111, 112, 113, 114, 115, 116, 117, 118, 119, 120, 121
Stalactites, 122, 123, 124, 125, 126, 127, 128, 129, 130, 131, 132, 133, 134, 135, 136, 137, 138, 139, 140, 141, 142, 143, 144, 145, 146, 147, 148, 149, 150

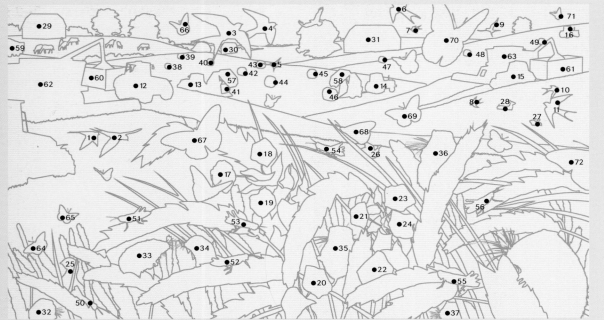

Wheat fields 16–17

Barn swallows, 1, 2, 3, 4, 5, 6, 7, 8, 9, 10, 11
Tractors, 12, 13, 14, 15, 16
Bindweed flowers, 17, 18, 19, 20, 21, 22, 23, 24
Ring-necked pheasants, 25, 26, 27
White-tailed deer, 28
Barns, 29, 30, 31
Fieldmice, 32, 33, 34, 35, 36, 37
Straw bales, 38, 39, 40, 41, 42, 43, 44, 45, 46, 47, 48, 49
Grasshoppers, 50, 51, 52, 53, 54, 55, 56
Baling machines, 57, 58
Grain trailers, 59, 60, 61
Combine harvesters, 62, 63
Monarch butterflies, 64, 65, 66, 67, 68, 69, 70, 71, 72

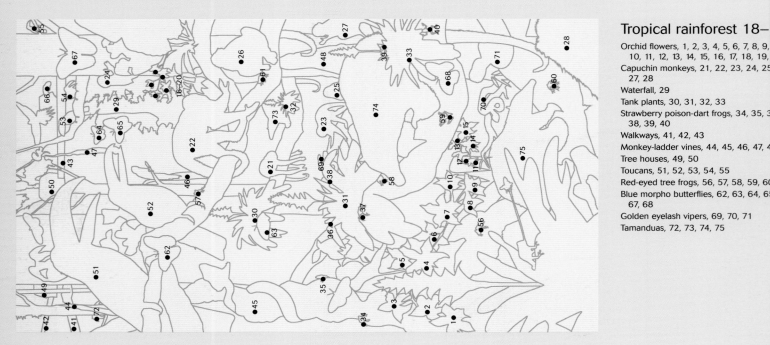

Tropical rainforest 18–19

Orchid flowers, 1, 2, 3, 4, 5, 6, 7, 8, 9, 10, 11, 12, 13, 14, 15, 16, 17, 18, 19, 20
Capuchin monkeys, 21, 22, 23, 24, 25, 26, 27, 28
Waterfall, 29
Tank plants, 30, 31, 32, 33
Strawberry poison-dart frogs, 34, 35, 36, 37, 38, 39, 40
Walkways, 41, 42, 43
Monkey-ladder vines, 44, 45, 46, 47, 48
Tree houses, 49, 50
Toucans, 51, 52, 53, 54, 55
Red-eyed tree frogs, 56, 57, 58, 59, 60, 61
Blue morpho butterflies, 62, 63, 64, 65, 66, 67, 68
Golden eyelash vipers, 69, 70, 71
Tamanduas, 72, 73, 74, 75

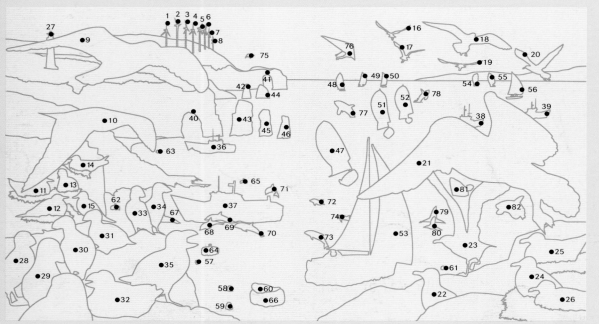

Craggy coast 20–21

Wind turbines, 1, 2, 3, 4, 5, 6, 7, 8
Herring gulls, 9, 10, 11, 12, 13, 14, 15, 16, 17, 18, 19, 20, 21, 22, 23, 24, 25, 26
Lighthouse, 27
Atlantic puffins, 28, 29, 30, 31, 32, 33, 34, 35
Trawlers, 36, 37, 38, 39
Arches, 40, 41
Stacks, 42, 43, 44, 45, 46
Yachts, 47, 48, 49, 50, 51, 52, 53, 54, 55, 56
Seals, 57, 58, 59, 60, 61
Mooring buoys, 62, 63, 64, 65, 66
Bottlenose dolphins, 67, 68, 69, 70, 71, 72, 73, 74
Hang-gliders, 75, 76
Killer whales, 77, 78, 79, 80, 81, 82

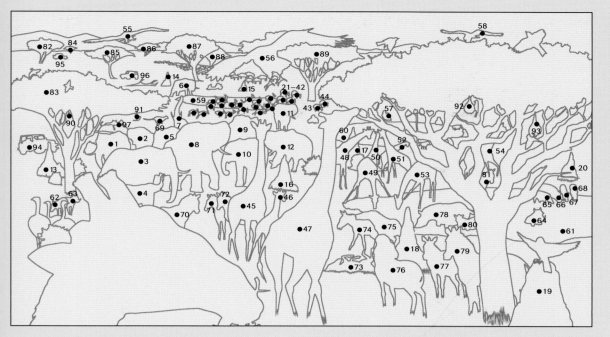

African grasslands 22–23

African elephants, 1, 2, 3, 4, 5, 6, 7, 8, 9, 10, 11, 12
Termite mounds, 13, 14, 15, 16, 17, 18, 19, 20
Springboks, 21, 22, 23, 24, 25, 26, 27, 28, 29, 30, 31, 32, 33, 34, 35, 36, 37, 38, 39, 40, 41, 42, 43, 44
Giraffes, 45, 46, 47, 48, 49, 50, 51, 52, 53, 54
Vultures, 55, 56, 57, 58
Water holes, 59, 60, 61
Warthogs, 62, 63, 64, 65, 66, 67, 68
Cheetah, 69
Zebras, 70, 71, 72, 73, 74, 75, 76, 77, 78, 79, 80, 81
Acacia trees, 82, 83, 84, 85, 86, 87, 88, 89
Weaverbird nests, 90, 91, 92, 93
Safari trucks, 94, 95, 96
Lions on a koppie, 97

Winding river 24–25

Green darner dragonflies, 1, 2, 3, 4, 5
Oxbow lake, 6
Wood ducks, 7, 8, 9, 10, 11, 12, 13
Painted turtles, 14, 15, 16, 17, 18, 19
Bridges, 20, 21
River otters, 22, 23, 24, 25, 26, 27, 28, 29, 30, 31
Water mill, 32
Blue flag iris flowers, 33, 34, 35, 36, 37, 38, 39, 40, 41, 42, 43, 44, 45, 46, 47, 48, 49, 50, 51, 52, 53
Great blue herons, 54, 55, 56, 57, 58
Brook silverside fish, 59, 60, 61, 62, 63
Water lily leaves, 64, 65, 66, 67, 68, 69, 70, 71, 72, 73, 74, 75, 76, 77, 78
Canoes, 79, 80
Yellow-spotted salamanders, 81, 82, 83

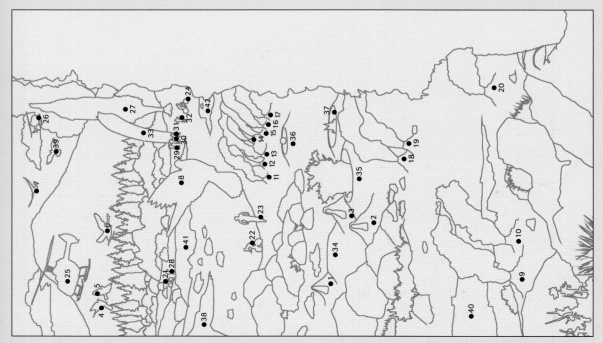

Hot spots 26–27

Mud volcanoes, 1, 2, 3
New Zealand wood pigeons, 4, 5, 6, 7, 8
Fumaroles, 9, 10, 11, 12, 13, 14, 15, 16, 17, 18, 19, 20
Cyclists, 21, 22, 23, 24
Helicopters, 25, 26
Geyser, 27
Tourists taking photographs, 28, 29, 30, 31, 32
Rainbow, 33
Mud pots, 34, 35, 36, 37
New Zealand falcons, 38, 39
Hot springs, 40, 41, 42

31

Index

Managing editor: Gillian Doherty
Additional design and DTP: Kerry Pearson, Natacha Goransky and Mike Olley
Editorial assistance: Fiona Patchett
Cartographic consultant: Craig Asquith

The publishers would like to thank the following people for their helpful advice:
Saki Daorana, manager for tourism, Qaanaaq Tourist Office, Greenland;
Katrina Knill, ranger, Department of Conservation, Ruapehu Area Office, New Zealand;
Darren Naish, School of Earth and Environmental Sciences, University of Portsmouth.

Pub. 15.95 8/10